THE OFFICIAL

MANCHESTER UNITED®

MATHS

BOOK 1

PAUL BROADBENT

Kick-off

The Manchester United books are a fun way to learn and practise your maths skills. Each book contains:
Theme visits to Manchester United, six Big Matches and a board game!

The 'theme' visits

Learn more about Manchester United and football.

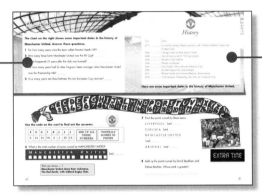

Enjoy the fun activities (*answers on pages 30–31*).

The Big Matches

Learn a new skill.

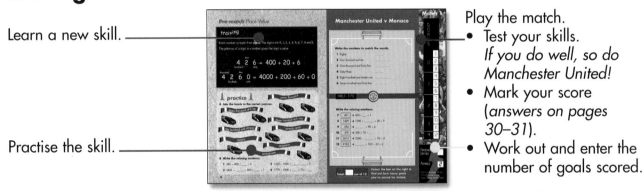

Practise the skill.

Play the match.
- Test your skills. *If you do well, so do Manchester United!*
- Mark your score (*answers on pages 30–31*).
- Work out and enter the number of goals scored.

After the match:
Enter each result on page 28. Work out Manchester United's league position!

The board game

What you need.

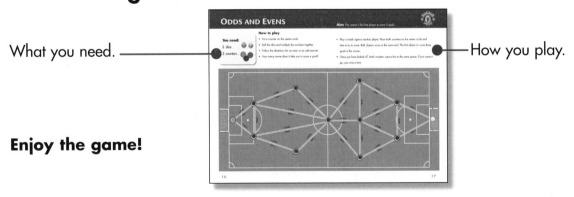

How you play.

Enjoy the game!

Contents

The chart on the right shows some important dates in the history of Manchester United. Answer these questions.

1 For how many years were the team called Newton Heath LYR? _____

2 How many times have Manchester United won the FA Cup? _____

3 What happened 31 years after the club was formed? _____

4 For how many years had Sir Alex Ferguson been manager when Manchester United won the Premiership title? _____

5 How many years are there between the two European Cup victories? _____

Use the code on the scarf to find out the answers.

F	O	O	T	B	A	L	L
6	15	15	20	2	1	12	12

ADD UP ALL THESE NUMBERS

'FOOTBALL' SCORES 83 POINTS

6 What is the total number of points scored by MANCHESTER UNITED?

M A N C H E S T E R   U N I T E D

Total _____

> **Did you know ... ?**
> Manchester United share their nickname, The Red Devils, with Salford Rugby Club.

History

Year	Event
1878	Formed as Newton Heath Lancashire and Yorkshire Railway Cricket and Football Club
1902	Changed name to Manchester United
1909	First of their record 10 FA Cup victories
1910	Moved to Old Trafford
1958	Munich air disaster
1968	First English club to win the European Cup
1986	Sir Alex Ferguson became manager
1993	Winners of the first Premier Division championship
1999	Treble winners: Premiership title, FA Cup, European Cup

Here are some important dates in the history of Manchester United.

N	O	P	Q	R	S	T	U	V	W	X	Y	Z
14	15	16	17	18	19	20	21	22	23	24	25	26

7 Find the points scored by these teams.

LIVERPOOL Total _____

CHELSEA Total _____

NEWCASTLE UNITED

Total _____

ARSENAL Total _____

EXTRA TIME

8 Add up the points scored by David Beckham and

Fabien Barthez. Whose total is greater?

_____

Pre-match Place Value

training

Every number is made from **digits**. The digits are 0, 1, 2, 3, 4, 5, 6, 7, 8 and 9.

The position of a digit in a number gives the digit a value.

$$\underset{\text{hundreds}}{4} \quad \overset{\text{tens}}{2} \quad \underset{\text{units}}{6} = 400 + 20 + 6$$

$$\overset{\text{thousands}}{4} \quad \underset{\text{hundreds}}{2} \quad \overset{\text{tens}}{6} \quad \underset{\text{units}}{0} = 4000 + 200 + 60 + 0$$

practice

A Join the boots to the correct scarves.

 seven thousand

 17   71

 seven thousand and ten

170     70

seven hundred and one

one hundred and seventy

seventy-seven

seventy    7010    7000

seventeen

701

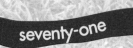 seventy-one    77

B Write the missing numbers.

1 $485 = 400 + \underline{\quad} + 5$

2 $1265 = 1000 + \underline{\quad} + \underline{\quad} + 5$

3 $2841 = \underline{\quad} + 800 + \underline{\quad} + 1$

4 $1779 = 1000 + \underline{\quad} + 70 + \underline{\quad}$

Manchester United v Monaco

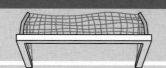

Write the numbers to match the words.

1 Eighty   _____

2 Four hundred and ten   _____

3 One thousand and forty-five   _____

4 Sixty-three   _____

5 Eight hundred and ninety-one   _____

6 Seven hundred and forty-two   _____

HALF-TIME

Write the missing numbers.

7   461 → 400 + ___ + 1

8   1429 → 1000 + _____ + 20 + 9

9   294 → _____ + 90 + 4

10   378 → 300 + 70 + ___

11   2614 → 2000 + _____ + 10 + 4

12   8152 → _____ + 100 + 50 + 2

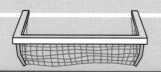

Total: ☐ **out of 12**

Colour the bar on the right to find out how many goals you've scored for United.

GOALS

GOALS	
	1
0	2
	3
	4
1	5
	6
	7
2	8
	9
	10
3	11
4	12

MANCHESTER UNITED ☐

MONACO **2**

Now turn to page 28 and fill in the score on the Super-League Results Table.

The Players

Do you share a birthday with any of these players?

HAPPY BIRTHDAY MANCHESTER UNITED!

GARY NEVILLE	18 FEBRUARY	DWIGHT YORKE	3 NOVEMBER
DENIS IRWIN	31 OCTOBER	OLE GUNNAR SOLSKJAER	26 FEBRUARY
DAVID MAY	24 JUNE	HENNING BERG	1 SEPTEMBER
RONNY JOHNSEN	10 JUNE	JESPER BLOMQVIST	5 FEBRUARY
JAAP STAM	17 JULY	WES BROWN	13 OCTOBER
DAVID BECKHAM	2 MAY	FABIEN BARTHEZ	28 JUNE
NICKY BUTT	21 JANUARY	LUKE CHADWICK	18 NOVEMBER
ANDY COLE	15 OCTOBER	QUINTON FORTUNE	21 MAY
TEDDY SHERINGHAM	2 APRIL	MIKAEL SILVESTRE	9 AUGUST
RYAN GIGGS	29 NOVEMBER	DAVID HEALY	5 AUGUST
PHIL NEVILLE	21 JANUARY	RONNIE WALLWORK	10 SEPTEMBER
MARK BOSNICH	13 JANUARY	JOHN O'SHEA	30 APRIL
ROY KEANE	10 AUGUST	ALEX NOTMAN	10 DECEMBER
RAIMOND VAN DER GOUW	24 MARCH	AND THE MANAGER...	
PAUL SCHOLES	16 NOVEMBER	SIR ALEX FERGUSON	31 DECEMBER

The grid shows the initials of some of the 2000/2001 squad.

	1	2	3	4	5	6	7	8	9	10
4	RG	PN	RW	RK	FB	DB	DY	RK	DI	MS
3	DB	JG	QF	DM	AC	RG	NB	RK	TS	LC
2	MB	GN	DI	PS	DY	JS	DB	NB	AC	DM
1	RG	JS	AC	RK	DB	PS	DY	OS	DW	WB

2 Ryan Giggs (RG) is at position (1,4). What other positions can you find him in?

_____

3 Can you find other players who are in more than two positions on the grid?

Give their names and positions. _____

_____

Month	Number of Birthdays					
	1	2	3	4	5	6
January						
February						
March						
April						
May						
June						
July						
August						
September						
October						
November						
December						

1 To find the most popular month for a Manchester United player to be born in, complete this bar chart.

4 Use the grid of players' initials to complete this crossword of their surnames.

Across
1 (1,2), 4 (6,2), 5 (9,2)
6 (7,4), 8 (6,1), 10 (4,3)
11 (10,1), 12 (1,1)

Down
1 (7,2), 2 (8,1), 3 (3,3)
7 (4,4), 9 (3,2)

5 Who is the hidden former Manchester United favourite? Rearrange the circled letters to find out

Pre-match Addition and Subtraction

practice

A Total these pairs.

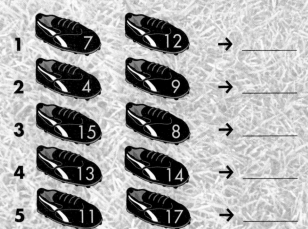

1 7   12   → _____
2 4   9   → _____
3 15 8   → _____
4 13 14   → _____
5 11 17   → _____

Find the difference between these pairs.

6   9   15   → _____

7   18   13   → _____

8   14    17   → _____

9   6   19   → _____

10   13   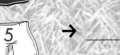 5   → _____

B 1 What is the sum of 5 and 13?

_____

2 What is the total of 7, 9 and 4?

_____

3 Which number is 6 less than 17?

_____

4 What is 19 subtract 5?

_____

Manchester United v Lazio

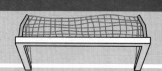

Work out these.

1 19 + 4 = _____

2 14 – 6 = _____

3 8 + 9 + 5 = _____

4 17 – 8 = _____

5 15 + 18 = _____

6 3 + 14 + 7 = _____

HALF-TIME

Try these.

7 What is the sum of 15 and 6? _____

8 Which number is 12 less than 20? _____

9 What is the total of 8, 9 and 10? _____

10 Mark and Anna spend 16p each. How much do they spend

altogether? _____

11 Sam has 14 badges and Jack has 7 more. How many badges

does Jack have? _____

12 Rebecca has 18 sweets. She eats 6 and gives 8 to David.

How many sweets does she have left? _____

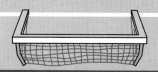

Total: [___] **out of 12**

Colour the bar on the right to find out how many goals you've scored for United.

GOALS

0	1
	2
	3
1	4
	5
	6
2	7
	8
	9
3	10
	11
4	12

MANCHESTER UNITED [___]

LAZIO **3**

Now turn to page 28 and fill in the score on the Super-League Results Table.

This was the first strip worn by
Newton Heath LYR in 1892.
The shirt shows two halves which
were in green and gold.

They were also the Manchester
United third strip colours in
1992/93.

Sorting out socks.

3 The socks scattered on the right are muddled up. Join the matching pairs.

4 Circle the socks to help you to work out these fractions.

a $\frac{1}{2}$ of 8 = _____

b $\frac{1}{4}$ of 12 = _____

c $\frac{1}{2}$ of 10 = _____

d $\frac{1}{3}$ of 12 = _____

e $\frac{1}{5}$ of 10 = _____

f $\frac{1}{4}$ of 4 = _____

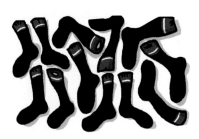  

Some football strips are designed in halves or in quarters.

1 Colour the designs on these kits to show halves and quarters.

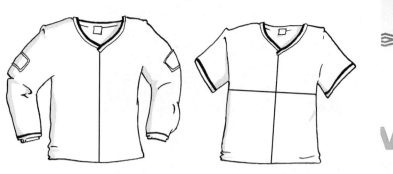

2 Colour the grids.

a Colour $\frac{1}{4}$ blue.

Colour $\frac{1}{4}$ red.

What fraction

is coloured? _____

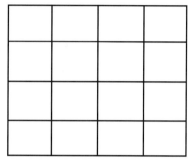

b Colour $\frac{1}{2}$ red.

Colour $\frac{1}{4}$ blue.

What fraction

is coloured? _____

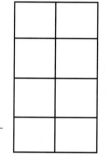

This is a strange strip. Do you think any Premier League teams would like to try it?

5 Complete the strip.

• Colour half the spots blue.

• Colour a quarter of them green.

• Colour the rest yellow.

• What fraction of the spots are yellow? _____

13

training

Look at this multiplication table.

×	0	1	2	3	4	5	6	7	8	9	10
2	0	2	4	6	8	10	12	14	16	18	20
5	0	5	10	15	20	25	30	35	40	45	50
10	0	10	20	30	40	50	60	70	80	90	100

5×4 is the same as 4×5.
It does not matter which way you multiply them.

practice

A Write the numbers that leave each turnstile.

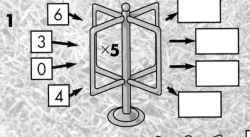

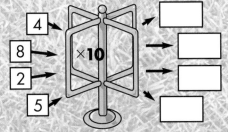

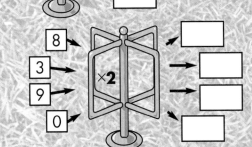

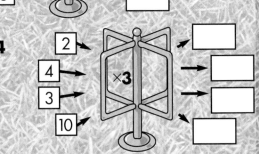

B Fill in the missing numbers.

1 $\boxed{} \times 3 = 15$

2 $8 \times \boxed{} = 16$

3 $5 \times 4 = \boxed{}$

4 $7 \times \boxed{} = 14$

5 $\boxed{} \times 3 = 12$

6 $7 \times 10 = \boxed{}$

Manchester United v Valencia

GOALS

Write the answers.

1 7 × 2 = _____
2 4 × 3 = _____
3 5 × 10 = _____
4 6 × 5 = _____
5 3 × 6 = _____
6 10 × 7 = _____

HALF-TIME

Write the missing numbers.

7 8 × ☐ = 16

8 ☐ × 5 = 20

9 9 × ☐ = 90

10 ☐ × 2 = 6

11 7 × ☐ = 14

12 ☐ × 3 = 21

GOALS	
0	1
	2
	3
1	4
	5
	6
2	7
	8
	9
3	10
	11
4	12

MANCHESTER UNITED ☐

VALENCIA 1

Now turn to page 28 and fill in the score on the Super-League Results Table.

Total: ☐ **out of 12**

Colour the bar on the right to find out how many goals you've scored for United.

ODDS AND EVENS

You need:

2 dice

3 counters

How to play

- Put a counter on the centre circle.

- Roll the dice and multiply the numbers together.

- Follow the directions for an even or an odd answer.

- How many moves does it take you to score a goal?

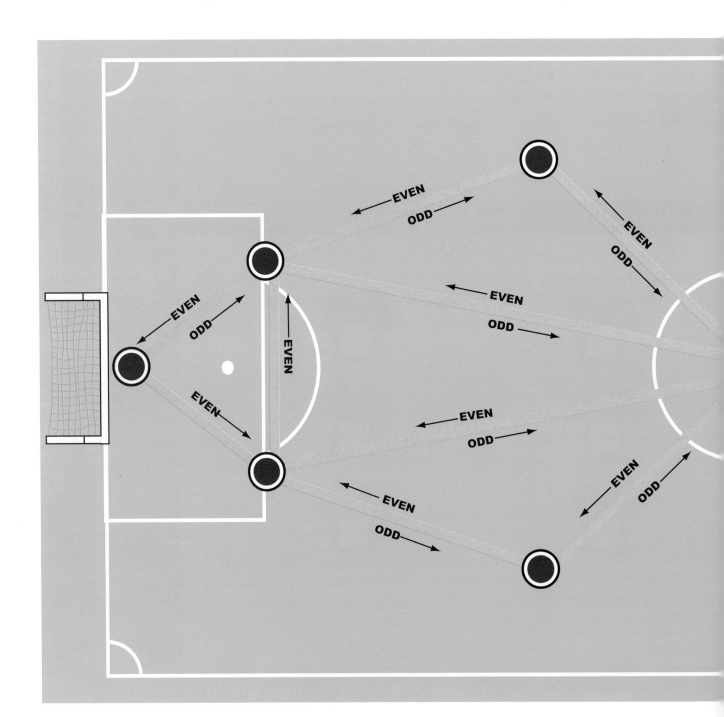

Aim: The winner is the first player to score 3 goals.

- Play a match against another player. Place both counters on the centre circle and take turns to move. Both players score at the same end. The first player to score three goals is the winner.

- Once you have kicked off, both counters cannot be in the same space. If you cannot go, you miss a turn.

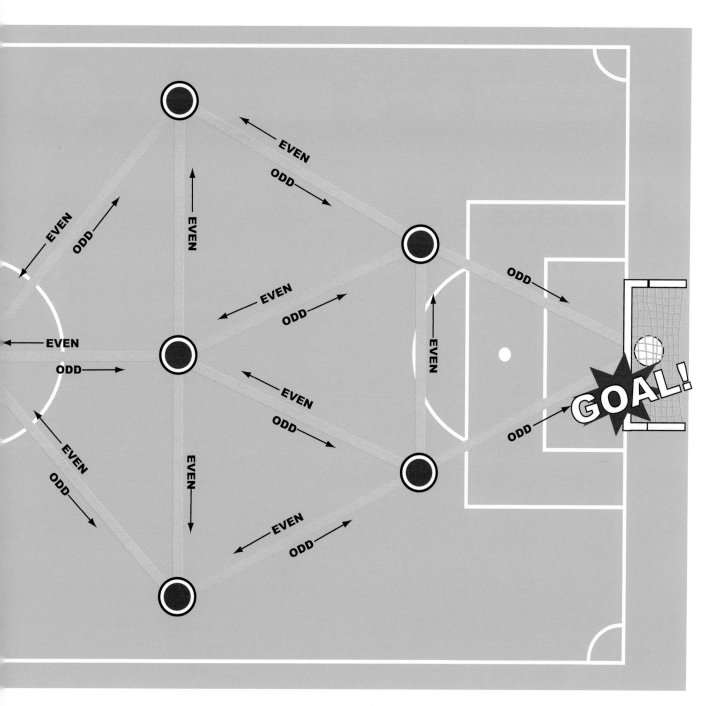

Pre-match Money

training

Working out **change** can be easy.
You must be able to make amounts up to £1.00.

A sticker costs 35p. This is how you can work out the change from £1.

35p → Make up to next 10p → + 5p → 40p → Make up to £1.00 → + 60p → change 65p

practice

A Write the totals.

1 [5p] [£10] [20p] = _____   2 [5p] [£10] [£20] [20p] = _____

3 [10p] [£10] [£10] [20p] = _____   4 [5p] [20p] [50p] [£10] = _____

Write the change.

5 [£10] price £7.50 = _____   6 [£5] price £3.75 = _____

7 [£2] price 90p = _____   8 [£1] price 85p = _____

B 1 Which three coins total 26p?   **2** Which three coins total 62p?

_____   _____

18

Manchester United v Bayern Munich

GOALS

0	1
	2
	3
	4
1	5
	6
2	7
	8
	9
	10
3	11
4	12

Write the totals.

1 £5.00 85p

2 30p 45p

3 20p 60p 35p

4 £10.00 £5.00 75p

5 85p 30p

6 40p 95p

HALF-TIME

Write the change from £1.00 for each of these prices.

7 55p _____

8 60p _____

9 85p _____

10 15p _____

11 30p _____

12 75p _____

Total: [ ] out of 12

Colour the bar on the right to find out how many goals you've scored for United.

MANCHESTER UNITED [ ]

BAYERN MUNICH 2

Now turn to page 28 and fill in the score on the Super-League Results Table.

Old Trafford

Old Trafford, the 'Theatre of Dreams', is the largest stadium in English football. It has recently been enlarged to accommodate 68 217 supporters.

Shapes can be spotted everywhere at Old Trafford.

rectangle

circle

rhombus

parallelogram

triangle

hexagon

square

semicircle

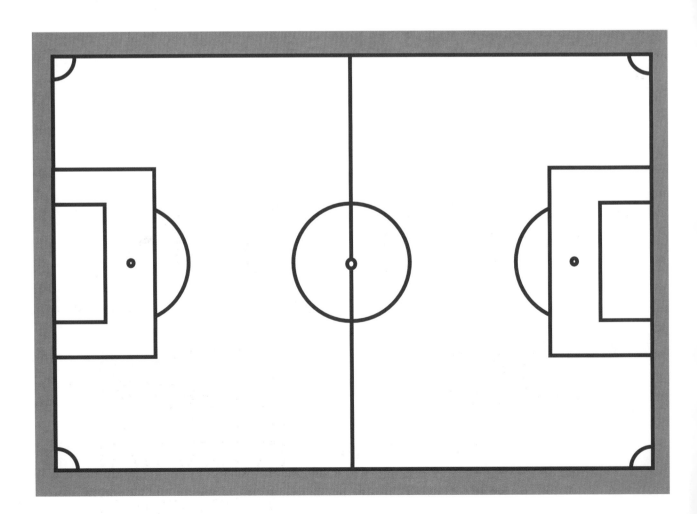

1 Name these shapes.

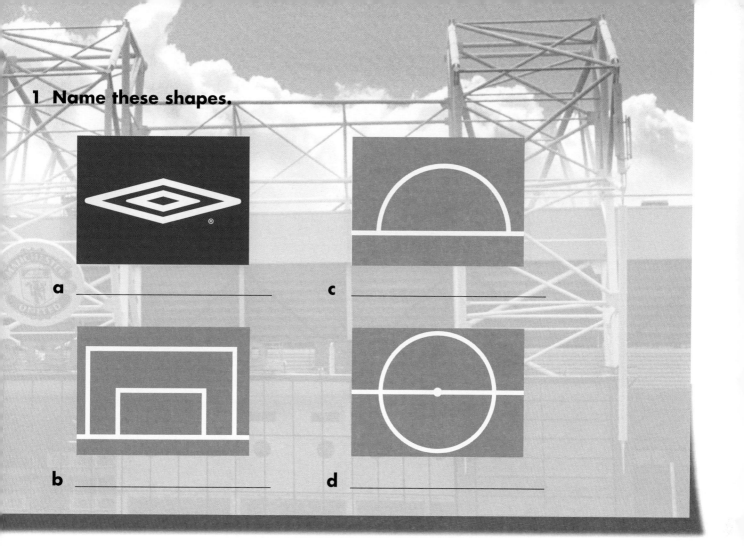

a _____

c _____

b _____

d _____

Look at the pitch on the left.

2 a Colour all the right angles on the pitch.

b How many right angles did you find? _____

3 Colour the right angles on these shapes.

Did you know ... ?
The roof of the North Stand is the largest in Europe. It is the same size as the football pitch.

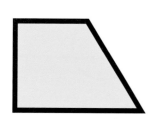 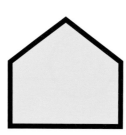 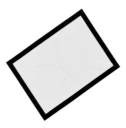 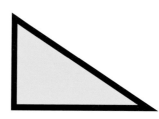

EXTRA TIME

4 Divide the grid into four parts. Each part must have one of each shape.

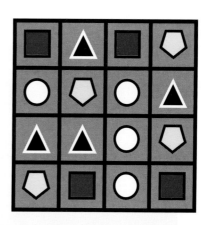

Pre-match Time

The **minute hand** tells you how many **minutes past the hour.**

o'clock

55 minutes past   5 minutes past

50 minutes past   10 minutes past

45 minutes past   15 minutes past

40 minutes past   20 minutes past

35 minutes past   25 minutes past

30 minutes past

practice

A Write the times shown on these clocks.

1

2

3

4

5

6

7

8

B Do you know these time facts?

1 How many minutes are in 1 hour? _____

2 How many days are there in April? _____

3 What time is half an hour before 4.15? _____

4 Which month follows October? _____

22

Manchester United v Ajax

GOALS

	1
0	2
	3
	4
1	5
	6
	7
2	8
	9
	10
3	11
4	12

Write the times.

1 _____minutes past _____

2 _____minutes past _____

3 _____minutes past _____

4 _____minutes past _____

5 _____minutes past _____

6 _____minutes past _____

HALF-TIME

Draw the hands on the clocks for these times.

7 4.05

8 9.35

9 2.45

10 11.20

11 6.55

12 8.15

MANCHESTER UNITED ☐

AJAX **1**

Total: ☐ **out of 12**

Colour the bar on the right to find out how many goals you've scored for United.

Now turn to page 28 and fill in the score on the Super-League Results Table.

Fred the Red

Fred the Red became the official Manchester United mascot in 1994. The timetable of a typical match day for Fred is shown on the right.

Use Fred's programme to answer these.

1 How many hours are there between Fred's arrival at the stadium

and changing into his strip? _____

2 How many minutes is Fred out on the pitch entertaining the fans? _____

3 What happens at half-past two? _____

4 How long is Fred at the stadium in total? _____

Fred is trying to work out how many goals he has scored!

5 Write in the signs (+ − × ÷) to help Fred get his sums correct.

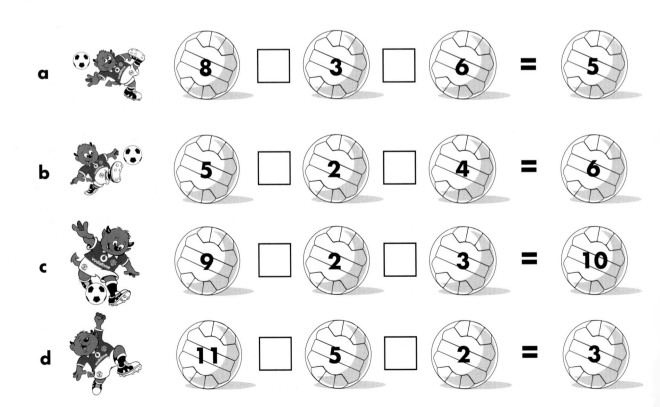

a   8 ☐ 3 ☐ 6 = 5

b   5 ☐ 2 ☐ 4 = 6

c   9 ☐ 2 ☐ 3 = 10

d   11 ☐ 5 ☐ 2 = 3

Fred's Programme

12.00	Arrives at stadium and has pre-match meal.
2.00	Changes into his strip.
2.30	Meets the children who are the match mascots.
2.45	Out on the pitch, entertains the fans.
2.55	Goes to entrance of players' tunnel to wait for the players.
3.00	Greets the players and then escorts the match mascots off the pitch.
3.45	At half-time, out on the pitch entertaining the fans.
4.00	Showers and changes out of strip.
4.45	Leaves the stadium and returns home.

+	4		9
7			16
11		19	
	18		

+	4		
	13	19	
6			
15			26

6 Write the missing numbers on these addition grids. Add the number in the red row to the number in the yellow column to fill in the blanks.

training

Rounding to the nearest 10

When you are rounding to the nearest 10, look at the **last digit**. If it is 5 or more, round up. If not, round down.

37 $\longrightarrow$ Round up to 40

144 $\longrightarrow$ Round down to 140

365 $\longrightarrow$ Round up to 370

Rounding to the nearest 100

When you are rounding to the nearest 100, look at the **last 2 digits**. If they make 50 or more, round up. If not, round down.

572 $\longrightarrow$ Round up to 600

839 $\longrightarrow$ Round down to 800

650 $\longrightarrow$ Round up to 700

practice

A Round each number to the nearest 10.

1 74 $\longrightarrow$ _____

2 96 $\longrightarrow$ _____

3 145 $\longrightarrow$ _____

4 307 $\longrightarrow$ _____

5 294 $\longrightarrow$ _____

Round each number to the nearest 100.

6 460 $\longrightarrow$ _____

7 348 $\longrightarrow$ _____

8 709 $\longrightarrow$ _____

9 850 $\longrightarrow$ _____

10 134 $\longrightarrow$ _____

B Read these scales. Round each one to the nearest 100 g.

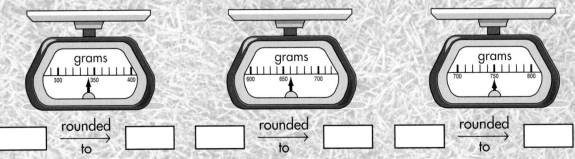

Manchester United v Malmo

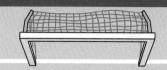

Round these to the nearest 10.

1 86 → _____

2 107 → _____

3 245 → _____

4 614 → _____

5 956 → _____

6 203 → _____

HALF-TIME

Round each scale to the nearest 100 g.

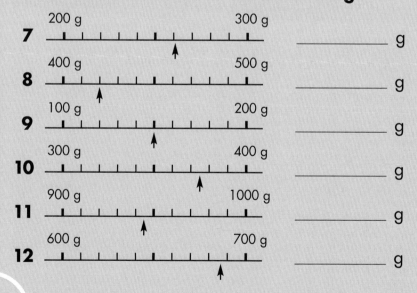

7 200 g — 300 g _____ g

8 400 g — 500 g _____ g

9 100 g — 200 g _____ g

10 300 g — 400 g _____ g

11 900 g — 1000 g _____ g

12 600 g — 700 g _____ g

Total: [ ] out of 12

Colour the bar on the right to find out how many goals you've scored for United.

GOALS

0	1
	2
	3
1	4
	5
	6
2	7
	8
	9
3	10
	11
4	12

MANCHESTER UNITED [ ]

MALMO **0**

Now turn to page 28 and fill in the score on the Super-League Results Table.

Super-League Results

MATCH 1

Man Utd	☐	Monaco	2
Malmo	3	Valencia	2
Lazio	0	Ajax	2

MATCH 2

Man Utd	☐	Lazio	3
Valencia	2	Monaco	2
Malmo	2	B Munich	2

MATCH 3

Valencia	1	Man Utd	☐
Lazio	1	Monaco	0
Ajax	4	B Munich	3

MATCH 4

B. Munich	2	Man Utd	☐
Valencia	1	Lazio	3
Malmo	0	Ajax	2

MATCH 5

Ajax	1	Man Utd	☐
B Munich	1	Lazio	1
Malmo	4	Monaco	0

MATCH 6

Man Utd	☐	Malmo	0
Monaco	0	Ajax	0
Valencia	0	B Munich	2

MATCH 7

B Munich	1	Monaco	3
Valencia	1	Ajax	1
Malmo	0	Lazio	1

Super-League Tables

Enter the score for each match.

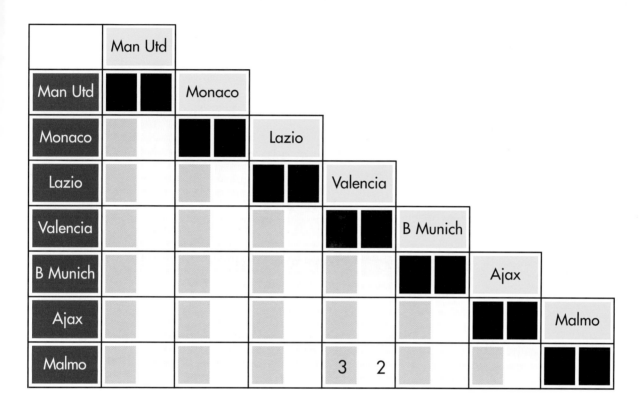

Complete the league table when all the matches are finished.

Win   3 pts   Draw   1 pt   Lose   0 pts

Team	Played	Won	Drew	Lost	For	Against	Goal diff	Points
Man Utd	6							
Monaco	6							
Lazio	6							
Valencia	6							
B Munich	6							
Ajax	6							
Malmo	6							

Champions [   ]   Runners-up [   ]

The Club 4–5
1 24 years **2** 10 **3** First FA Cup victory
4 7 years **5** 31 years **6** 179
7 Liverpool – 124; Chelsea – 53
   Newcastle United – 175; Arsenal – 70
8 Fabien Barthez's score was greater – 117.
   David Beckham scored 83.

Match 1 Place Value 6–7

Pre-match.
A 7000 seven thousand
   17 seventeen
   71 seventy-one
   701 seven hundred and one
   77 seventy-seven
   7010 seven thousand and ten
   170 one hundred and seventy
   70 seventy
B 1 80 **2** 200, 60 **3** 2000, 40 **4** 700, 9

The Match
1 80 **2** 410 **3** 1045 **4** 63 **5** 891 **6** 742
7 60 **8** 400 **9** 200 **10** 8 **11** 600
12 8000

The Players 8–9
1 November
2 (1,1) (6,3)
3 David Beckham (1,3) (5,1) (6,4) (7,2)
   Andy Cole (3,1) (5,3) (9,2)
   Roy Keane (4,1) (4,4) (8,3) (8,4)
   Dwight Yorke (5,2) (7,1) (7,4)
4 Across 1 Bosnich 4 Stam 5 Cole 6 Yorke
   8 Scholes 10 May 11 Brown 12 Giggs
   Down 1 Beckham 2 Solskjaer 3 Fortune
   7 Keane 9 Irwin
5 Cantona

Match 2 Addition and Subtraction ...10–11
Pre-match
A 1 19 **2** 13 **3** 23 **4** 27 **5** 28 **6** 6 **7** 5
   8 3 **9** 13 **10** 8
B 1 18 **2** 20 **3** 11 **4** 14

The Match
1 23 **2** 8 **3** 22 **4** 9 **5** 33 **6** 24 **7** 21
8 8 **9** 27 **10** 32p **11** 21 **12** 4

The Strip 12–13
1 Check the colouring shows halves and
   quarters.
2 a $\frac{1}{2}$ **b** $\frac{3}{4}$
3 Check the socks are matched correctly.
4 a 4 **b** 3 **c** 5 **d** 4 **e** 2 **f** 1
5 $\frac{1}{4}$ are yellow

Match 3 Multiplication Tables 14–15
Pre-match
A 1 30 15 0   20
   2 40 80 20 50
   3 16 6   18 0
   4 6   12 9   30
B 1 5 **2** 2 **3** 20 **4** 2 **5** 4 **6** 70

The Match
1 14 **2** 12 **3** 50 **4** 30 **5** 18 **6** 70
7 2 **8** 4 **9** 10 **10** 3 **11** 2 **12** 7

Match 4 Money 18–19
Pre-match
A 1 £10.25 **2** £30.25 **3** £20.30 **4** £10.75
   5 £2.50 **6** £1.25 **7** £1.10 **8** 15p
B 1 20p coin, 5p coin and 1p coin
   2 50p coin, 10p coin and 2p coin

The Match
1 £5.85 **2** 75p **3** £1.15 **4** £15.75
5 £1.15 **6** £1.35 **7** 45p **8** 40p **9** 15p
10 85p **11** 70p **12** 25p

Old Trafford 20–21
1 a Rhombuses **b** Rectangles **c** Semicircle
   d Circle
2 a Check the right angles. **b** 32
3

4

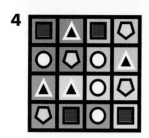

Match 5 Time 22–23

Pre-match

A 1 5 minutes past 5 **2** 55 minutes past 9
  3 30 minutes past 8 **4** 40 minutes past 2
  5 5 minutes past 3 **6** 35 minutes past 3
  7 8 o'clock **8** 45 minutes past 5
B 1 60 minutes **2** 30 days **3** 3.45
  4 November

The Match

1 15 minutes past 4
2 35 minutes past 8
3 45 minutes past 6
4 10 minutes past 11
5 55 minutes past 1
6 40 minutes past 2

7  **8**   **9**

10   **11**   **12**

Fred the Red 24–25

1 2 hours **2** 25 minutes
3 Meets the children who are the
  match mascots.
4 4 hours 45 minutes
5 a + –
  b × –
  c – +
  d – ÷

6

+	4	8	9
7	11	15	16
11	15	19	20
14	18	22	23

+	4	10	11
9	13	19	20
6	10	16	17
15	19	25	26

Match 6

Rounding and Reading Scales 26–27

Pre-match

A 1 70 **2** 100 **3** 150 **4** 310 **5** 290
  6 500 **7** 300 **8** 700 **9** 900 **10** 100
B 340 g 300 g; 660 g 700 g;
  750 g 800 g

The Match

1 90 **2** 110 **3** 250 **4** 610 **5** 960
6 200 **7** 300 g **8** 400 g **9** 200 g
10 400 g **11** 900 g **12** 700 g

Collect the set

Each book introduces new skills and harder challenges. Collect all 16 and be an English and Maths champion.

Manchester United English   Louis Fidge

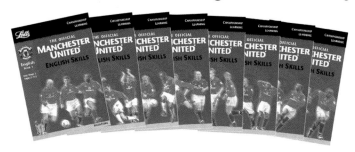

Manchester United Maths   Paul Broadbent

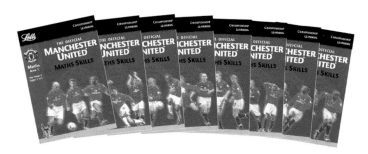

Manchester United Plc, Sir Matt Busby Way, Old Trafford, Manchester M16 0RA

Letts Educational, Aldine House, Aldine Place, London W12 8AW
Tel: 020 8740 2266 Fax: 020 8743 8451 E-mail: mail@lettsed.co.uk
Website: www.letts-education.com